FIRST MEASURES
OF THE COMING
INSURRECTION

ABOUT THE AUTHORS

Eric Hazan is a writer, historian and founder of
the independent publishing house La Fabrique.
His most recent books in English include
The Invention of Paris (2012) and *A People's
History of the French Revolution* (2014).

Kamo are a group of anonymous
French revolutionaries.

FIRST MEASURES OF THE COMING INSURRECTION

Eric Hazan and Kamo

Translated by Patrick Camiller

Zed Books

LONDON

First Measures of the Coming Insurrection
was first published in English in 2015 by Zed Books Ltd,
Unit 2.8, The Foundry, 17 Oval Way,
London, SE11 5RR, UK

www.zedbooks.co.uk

Typeset in Adobe Garamond Pro by seagulls.net
Cover designed by Dougal Burgess

A catalogue record for this book is available
from the British Library

ISBN 978-1-78360-409-8 pb
ISBN 978-1-78360-411-1 pdf
ISBN 978-1-78360-412-8 epub
ISBN 978-1-78360-413-5 mobi

Printed and bound by CPI Group (UK) Ltd, Croydon, CR0 4YY

CONTENTS

A MOMENT TO BRING
US UP TO DATE

As the final revisions were being made to the French edition of this book, Turkey was ablaze on account of a few dozen trees set to vanish under a government property development project. Scarcely had the repression struck Taksim Gezi Park in Istanbul when it was Brazil's turn to enter the fray, this time because of a small rise in bus fares. Hundreds of thousands of demonstrators took to the streets, even invading Brasília, attacking parliament with Molotov cocktails, ransacking banks, routing the police, and disturbing the mindless reign of football.

For at least three years now, such explosions have been continually interrupting the refrain of the 'end of history' and disproving all the editorial commentators. Were they not celebrating on French radio and TV, just a week before the revolt, the huge benefits that the Brazilian people would gain from the organization of the World Cup?

We are living through an upheaval of historic proportions. The visible evidence of collapse makes criticism redundant. What is being born before our eyes still lacks a clear shape; it could just as easily beget monsters and therefore defies any attempt to describe it. In such times, all commentary is reduced to the level of chit-chat. We can speak only from the midst of events; from the breach we can hear the cracking foundations of a global order at its end that are opening up new paths for the future.

The modest aim of this book is to reopen the question of revolution. It does not hold forth on the present catastrophe or demonstrate 'scientifically' the inevitable breakdown of capitalism; nor does it speculate on whether an uprising is just around the corner. The coming insurrection is our starting point – what it ushers in, not what it draws a line under.

The last revolutionary wave, in the 1960s and 1970s, had its certitudes and illusions, its distinctive language and programmes. In May 1968, the most resolute fringes of the movement had a clear idea of what 'people's emancipation' meant in practice: factory self-management, workers' councils, dictatorship of the proletariat, technological progress, and all the time and energies that that progress would make possible. Much in those themes was metabolized by the neoliberal reaction of the eighties and nineties. Today we must find new points of support.

We put forward no programme, except perhaps to get our hands dirty and to investigate the strange mechanism of revolution. What means should be deployed to become, and above all to remain, ungovernable? What should be done to ensure that things do not slam shut again on the day after the insurrection, that the newly won liberty becomes more extensive? Or, in other words, what means are appropriate for our ends?

Some will see behind this ambition either senile nostalgia or the mindless elation of youth. But let them take comfort, as much as they can. We are sure of being the most realistic by far.

1

IT IS RIGHT TO REBEL

It is therefore madness without equal

To try to involve ourselves in correcting the world.

Molière, *The Misanthrope*, Act 1, Scene 1

Right across this planet, there are three basic kinds of government under which people live. In the first, a particular group (often called a party) holds all the power, elections are rigged, the media are muzzled, and opponents are behind bars or vanish without trace. It is a situation that applies in many former or present 'communist' countries and in others that have emerged from colonial rule and continue their past rulers' brutality in various guises. In the second category, the regime is unstable and threatened with stones or guns – as in today's Syria or the Democratic Republic of Congo. The third type comprises what are usually called 'democracies': elections take place at fixed dates, parliaments adopt laws, and governments *manage* public affairs. The richest countries periodically send their leaders to discuss the future of the world at secure places cordoned off by large numbers of police. The rest receive heaps of praise when they show that they have assimilated 'democratic' values while accepting the plunder of their resources and the reduction of their people to beggars.

The boundaries between these categories are not always sharply drawn: some major countries – Algeria, Iran, Russia – have features of both the first and the third, while others can pass suddenly from one to another, as Mubarak's Egypt did recently from the first to the second. And the countries of the 'Bolivarian revolution' – Venezuela, Ecuador, Bolivia – form something like a group of their own, in which some are willing to place their hopes.

Over time a zone of obligatory deference has formed around the word 'democracy'. Born at the heart of the West, it is a system of government that helps the rest of the world to join in by various means. All leaders, from the most emollient social democrats to the worst despots, feel compelled to affirm their attachment to democracy. It is incontestable because it is the regime of liberty, which an insidious shift then identifies with liberal values, free trade, free competition and neoliberalism. Since the end of the 'people's democracies', now a baneful memory, democracy has been inseparable from capitalism in its various aliases, and we shall therefore speak in this text of *democratic capitalism*.

Democratic capitalism has imposed itself as the ultimate, definitive form of social existence, not only in the ideology of the ruling class but even in the popular imagination. But its legitimacy rests on a tripod, each of whose legs is worm-eaten or seriously cracked. The first is the constant rise in living standards supposedly leading to the formation of a universal middle class – a process that first took shape with Fordism (wage increases in line with productivity, so that the workers can buy more and keep the wheels of industry turning) and the different variants of social democracy since the New Deal, the Popular

Front and postwar British labourism. Today, that pillar exists only in the head: that is, in the forecasts of finance ministries and international agencies, which are constantly belied by the facts and keep being revised downwards despite all the massaging of figures.

The second pillar is the peace that capitalism is supposed to have brought to the planet after 'the horrors of the first half of the twentieth century'. One need scarcely be an expert in geopolitics, however, to see wars all around us: civil wars of an intensity that varies according to time and place (muted in Europe, fierce in the Middle East); terrible African wars against a backdrop of minerals, diamonds and famine; forgotten guerrilla wars in Burma and the Philippines; never-ending wars in Afghanistan, Somalia and Palestine. Are all those wars tribal, ethnic and religious? Behind each one, democratic capitalism is busy defending its economic and strategic interests, its oil, mining and agribusiness. Democratic capitalism has lost all credibility as the great pacifier, as the global Leviathan.

The most rotten of the three pillars is 'democratic legitimacy' based on universal suffrage. After all, nations are led by the men and women the people have elected, and if they are unhappy they have only to choose others the next time round. François Arago, an old Republican, already put forward this argument when he was shelling the barricades in the Latin Quarter in June 1848: universal suffrage has spoken, the people should not take up arms against those it has chosen.

But despite the etymology, despite the articles of constitutions asserting the sovereignty of the people, power nowhere belongs to the *demos*. That has been evident for a long time, but now there is something new as well. Today, power does not belong either to the caste of politicians who, by tradition, allocate ministerial and administrative posts to themselves in accordance with an electoral timetable. That kind of politics is no longer more than an empty form. Since 'the crisis', the masked reality lying unsaid beneath the surface has appeared in the light of day: the economy is directly political; power, to use the coy formula, is nothing other than 'the power of the markets', whose fears, whims and demands are expressed in banner headlines and commented on by all manner of experts (the expert being the emblematic figure of our times). *Markets:* that sounds reassuring. What is more peaceful than going to the market? The word maintains anonymity with regard to what it covers up, disguising all the aspects through which we participate in our own dispossession. We often read in the newspapers that 'the markets are worried', or even 'alarmed'. The public reaction would probably be less placid, less resigned, if things were spelled out clearly: those who are unhappy or alarmed are the directors of major banks and insurance companies, the managers of funds – not only pension funds but also speculative 'hedge funds', private equity funds – and the totally unregulated 'shadow banking system'.

There may be clashes of interest among the components of private finance, but these still form a single totality ('the markets') since all their top personnel have certain opinions in common. Trained in the same school of thought, reading the same texts, meeting in the same forums, they share the same vision of what is good for the world, and especially for themselves.

Moreover, there is a complete osmosis between private finance and national governments, central banks and the European Commission. This involves a dual mechanism of highly official lobbying and revolving doors. In France, the big career move for finance ministry inspectors is to join the top echelons of private banks, with a tenfold or twentyfold salary increase. This explains, for example, the shameful retreat of the Socialist government from Hollande's electoral promise of banking reform – a policy that was supposed to separate 'investment business' from deposit account functions, so that money belonging to savers would no longer be mixed up with the toxic sums resulting from financial deregulation. But the finance inspectors who planned its implementation were not keen to upset their future employers. Money in deposit accounts will therefore continue to cushion the speculative disasters of liberalized finance.

'The markets' have come to take direct control of the most highly indebted countries. In order to ensure that Greece remains in the eurozone, the 'troika' (European Union + International Monetary Fund + European Central Bank) has established there its own de facto rule that does not respect even the appearances of democracy. Cyprus recently suffered the same fate, and Portugal, Spain and Italy are under the supervision of this new Holy Alliance. If 'the crisis' reveals anything, it is less the greed of 'the markets' than the *political* subjection of all countries to the logic of economics.

In France, the beginning of the break-up of the established regime can be dated to the moment, in 1983, when the Socialists made their turn to *la rigueur*: that is, when they decided that the job of government was no more than to go with the flow of things. It was thus a Socialist (the late Pierre Bérégovoy) who organized the deregulation of finance in 1986. Since then, successive governments have merely taken note of the degradation in the material and subjective areas under their charge, content to create ministries whose names alone – 'recovery of production', 'national identity', 'economic solidarity', 'regional equality' – seem designed to ward off reality.

To say that the resulting system is cynical, unjust and brutal is not enough. To protest, demonstrate or petition is to accept by implication that improvements are possible *in the face of the crisis.* But what is called 'the crisis' is an essential political tool for management of the productive population as well as of those surplus to requirements. The discourse of crisis has spread in all the industrial countries and is constantly relayed by the media and the state apparatuses. 'Combating the crisis' and 'waging war on terror' naturally go hand in hand, both being based on the same elemental reflex, the fear of chaos.

After all the cheap credit to keep the poor quiet, after the bursting of various financial bubbles in the wake of soaring debt, 'the markets' are now demanding austerity in the hope that it will allow them to recover their stake at the expense of the general population (a process known as 'return to financial equilibrium'). Governments adopt the famous Thatcherite formula TINA (There Is No Alternative) and follow the directives of 'the markets', using the spectre of catastrophe to blackmail people into *the necessary sacrifices*.

People are not fooled, however; the patter of economists arouses nothing but jeers. One summit meeting after another, held to overcome 'the crisis', is greeted with striking indifference. Hatred of the Brussels bureaucracy is general, as is contempt for domestic politicians of every stripe. 'Domestic': yes, that's a good term for the garrulous staff in charge of running the everyday affairs of the country, with the servile task of getting everyone to accept the decisions taken by the real masters.

Scorned and hated though it is, democratic capitalism is not seriously under attack. There is talk of correcting its defects, making it fairer, more bearable, more 'ethical' – which is contrary to its operating principle, especially since the 'handling' of the crisis is based on low wages and organized insecurity. Nowhere is there any question of exposing it to the fate of oppressive regimes in the past, of seeing it off once and for all.

Nothing can be expected of the far left, whose rhetoric has been inaudible for a long time now; its vitality is exhausted, its idea of happiness completely deadly. Its worthiest militants – those who will join the right side when the time comes – no longer really believe in the fossilized Trotskyism common to most of the far left organizations and grouplets. They are where they are out of loyalty, *faute de mieux*, waiting for something to turn up. In France, the bragging of the Parti de gauche [PG; Left Party] has a certain echo, but its members will soon realize that to sing the Marseillaise, to don the

Phrygian cap and to dismiss banlieue rebels as fools does not amount to a programme, any more than Gambetta can be said to resemble Blanqui.

The *indignados* and the Occupy movement led to a certain awareness among types of individual who until then had been politically somnolent. That was not insignificant but hardly earth-shaking: democratic capitalism has seen their like before, and anyway it regards such movements with benevolent amusement.

The riots or near-riotous demonstrations in France, England, Greece and Sweden were less well received. On the right, the image was of hooligans mainly bent on looting fashionable stores. On the left, the emphasis was on the lack of political thinking behind the events. Such rejection is a sign of unease – justified, moreover, because those responsible for keeping order know where such popular bursts of energy might lead if they were organized and coordinated. It was to avoid the latter that, in all the 'democratic' countries, unusually severe sentences were handed down to 'ringleaders' chosen at random, in emergency conditions that had nothing in common with basic legality.

In the last few years, a number of discussion meetings have been held in London and Paris around 'the idea of communism'. The books that came out of them are useful, since they have helped to make it possible again to utter the word *communism* without apologizing for it. But, unless we are mistaken, the aim has never been seriously to propose the overthrow of democratic capitalism, to work *here and now* for the revolution (another word under a curse). Faced with an intolerable system that is cracking at the seams, this silence or strange absence is a feature of the present situation that deserves special consideration.

Reasons of a psychological or even anthropological nature have often been advanced to explain the seeming patience of the population: the privatization of existence, the transformation of 'people' into self-entrepreneurs, is supposed to have depoliticized the masses and to have made any prospect of revolutionary change illusory. The idea is not new: Castoriadis noted that 'in the societies of modern capitalism, political activity properly so called is tending to disappear', that 'radical political conflict is more and more disguised, stifled, deflected, and ultimately nonexistent' ('The Suspension of Publication of *Socialisme ou Barbarie*', June 1965). Shortly afterwards, the barricades on rue Gay-Lussac in Paris showed what should be thought of that.

Another explanation for the 'apathy' is globalization: since all countries are caught in the web of the planet-wide economy, it serves no purpose to get worked up in one particular corner; the web will swiftly quell any movement of local revolt through the simple force of inertia that a large whole imposes on its constituent parts. Probably this was the kind of argument that the ageing Metternich chewed over on his way into exile, concealed in a laundress's wagon. With the countries of Europe firmly set in the cement of the Holy Alliance, he thought, the fall of Louis Philippe should never have unleashed fire and blood across the continent; it was against all logic that the springtime of the peoples, in March 1848, should have hurled duchies and kingdoms around like playthings, all the way from Denmark to Sicily.

To blame globalization for people's 'listlessness' today is to treat them as a collective idiot, to display ignorance of history and present realities, to forget the serial collapse of Arab regimes known for the efficiency of their police and the loyalty of their armies.

In the desolate world of democratic capitalism, the insurrection will not fail to envelop the whole rickety structure of Europe, whether it starts out in Spain or Greece, France or Italy. The transmission will take place not by contagion – revolution is not an infectious pathogen – but by the effect of a shock wave, as the late lamented John Foster Dulles, father of the celebrated domino theory, once foresaw. The countries one might consider more stable – by virtue of their traditions, their apparent good health

or their distance from the epicentre – will be para-
lysed as the wave advances: the reasons why it is right
to rebel are so numerous, and have been evident for
so long, that no government will find the legitimacy
enabling it to crush the insurrection by brute force.
One success will bring others in its wake; the bold-
ness of some will increase tenfold the preparedness of
their neighbours to act.

What we must try to understand is not
some (nonexistent) 'depoliticization' but the prevail-
ing scepticism about the idea of revolution. The very
word, happily trotted out to sing the praises of a
new vacuum cleaner, arouses pitying smiles when it
is used to speak of the overthrow of the established
order. One of the reasons for this has to do with the
demise of barracks communism. To be sure, the leaders of the Soviet Union had long appeared as a gang
of brutal bureaucrats, and life in that country as an
unenviable fate, so that nothing much changed in
that respect when the end came in 1989. As Mario
Tronti summed it up in *La politica al tramonto* (Turin

1998), 'three years, from 1989 to 1991, were needed to confirm bureaucratically a death that had already occurred some time before. The socialist systems outlived the end of socialism.' Nevertheless, however aberrant the form of social organization in the USSR and the 'people's democracies', it liked to think of itself as different and claimed to be standing up to American imperialism. Deeply implanted in many a head was the idea that communism might have succeeded in different hands and in different circumstances. But that disappeared at the same time as the Soviet regime itself. The void that this created was like a period of mourning: you can feel relieved at the departure of a loathsome being yet also feel his absence as a lack. And all of a sudden the idea of revolution, linked to a whole set of images from the Smolny Institute and the *Aurora* cruiser, through Mayakovsky's voice and the communal housing designed by constructivist architects, to Eisenstein's *October* and Trotsky's armoured train, found itself buried along with 'actually existing socialism'.

At the same time, the *word* revolution is everywhere – in Peugeot publicity brochures as well as the tweets of *indignados* – so much so that it covers over our relationship to past revolutions. These constitute neither a tradition to uphold, nor a series of events to commemorate, but are the historical ground on which we stand. You can't find your way in an epoch unless you have learned of its revolutionary setbacks – those which led to defeats, and especially those which followed the victories.

In March 1789 a subject of Louis XVI would have been highly sceptical if someone had spoken to him of revolution, assuming that he even understood what was at issue. He would have agreed that the situation was worrying, that the state coffers were empty, that debt interest was soaking up half of the money coming in, that 2 per cent of the population owned the vast majority of the wealth, and that those privileged ones paid virtually nothing in taxes. He would have sighed at such great inequality and oppression.

But the throne – once sat upon by Clovis, Saint Louis, Henri IV and Louis XIV – probably seemed to him more everlasting than the market economy does to people today. As Camille Desmoulins put it a few years later: 'In 1789 there were not even ten of us republicans.'

2

CREATING THE IRREVERSIBLE

Definitions of basic historical concepts:
Catastrophe – to have missed the opportunity.
Critical moment – the status quo threatens
to be preserved. Progress – the first
revolutionary measure taken.
Walter Benjamin, *The Arcades Project*

Today, in a country like France, the conditions are present for a *meltdown of the regime* under the impact of an uprising and a general jamming of the system, as described in *L'insurrection qui vient* (La Fabrique, 2007; English translation: *The Coming Insurrection*, Semiotext(e), 2009). The phenomenon has already occurred twice in the history of France. The first time was the summer of 1789: when news spread far and wide of the capture of the Bastille, the governmental structure inherited from Richelieu and Colbert spontaneously broke up. The *intendants* – representatives of the centre, equivalent to today's prefects – simply packed up and quit their posts, leaving the keys in the door, and the constitutional bodies of the state (parliaments and municipalities, whose members drew their power from heredity, venality or direct appointment by the centre) dissolved along with them. There did remain an executive, a king and ministers, but they no longer ran anything; the driving belt was broken beyond repair.

The second meltdown took place in May 1968, when the Gaullist regime vanished in the face of a student revolt and the largest strike the country had ever seen. Of course the vacuum lasted only a few days: it was all so sudden, so unexpected, that no one was mentally prepared to take advantage of the exceptional situation. Much more than the CRS riot police, Prefect Grimaud or the threats of General Massu, this lack at the level of theory and programme, which the wild imaginings of Trotskyists and Maoists did not fill, enabled the Communist Party and the CGT [General Confederation of Labour] to get things back under control, with the result that Gaullism was able to re-emerge triumphant in June.

Recently, Ben Ali and Mubarak also vanished into thin air despite the police and special forces they had at their disposal – in countries thought to be 'depoliticized' by decades of dictatorship. But no thought had been given to how those magnificent popular uprisings should be followed up. For want of preparation, the opportunity to put an end to the old order was not taken, so that in Tunisia as well as Egypt a 'constitutional process' got under way to reshuffle the pack without a decisive break: a self-proclaimed provisional government reined in the revolutionary movement, then organized elections that reintroduced – or will introduce – another dire selection of old-regime notables. And all this was done with the blessing of the West, increasingly reassured as the spectre of a genuine Arab revolution faded away.

This is not new. The sequence *popular government – provisional government – elections – reaction* may be found numerous times in history. In February 1848, in the hours following the abdication of Louis Philippe, a group of deputies around Lamartine proclaimed itself the provisional government. They hastily organized the election of an Assembly which, in June, gave Cavaignac full powers to crush the proletarian insurgents, and then to promote the irresistible rise of Louis Bonaparte. On 4 September 1870, after the inglorious debacle of the Second Empire, the republic was proclaimed under popular pressure, but a provisional government of 'national defence' took over at the Hôtel de Ville in the French capital, organized the election of an assembly mainly consisting of rural deputies, got Paris to capitulate to the Prussian army, and gave Thiers full powers to crush the Paris Commune. In the German revolution of 1918–19, the provisional government of Friedrich Ebert, a Socialist, organized elections and crushed the Spartacist revolt and the Bavarian revolution, with the help of the Freikorps. In France during the Liberation, the provisional government set up by de Gaulle on his own authority proceeded to disarm the Resistance, to neutralize the popular movement and to get a Constituent Assembly elected which gave rise to the Fourth Republic – that is, the same mishmash as the Third Republic, only worse. The same scenario unfolded in Italy after the civil war of 1944–5.

In getting an assembly (usually qualified as 'constituent') elected at great speed, a provisional government wins on two counts. On the one hand, it establishes a fragile legitimacy that it cannot be sure of enjoying while it is still *self-proclaimed*: it shows that its intentions are pure, that it does not intend to hang on to power. On the other hand, it prevents 'extremists' from using the time they need to spread their ideas. The population, long fed the propaganda of the regime that has just been overthrown, will vote 'the right way', and the resulting Assembly will have the same colours as (or be even more reactionary than) the Chamber in place before the revolution. Blanqui, after February 1848, had these fears in mind when he called for the elections to be postponed, whereas the provisional government was determined to force the pace, rightly counting on the return of a parliament dominated by royalists and right-wing republicans.

The need to avoid this disastrous sequence at all costs was well understood by the most lucid of the demonstrators who surrounded the parliament in Madrid on 25 September 2012. To the slogan of 'proceso constituyente', they counterposed that of a 'marea destituyente', a disaggregating tidal wave.

The most difficult step, and the most contrary to 'common sense', is to shake off the idea that a *transition period* is indispensable between before and after, between the old regime and active emancipation. Since the country must continue to function, we'll keep the old administrative and police structures, we'll keep the social machinery running on the pivots of work and the economy, we'll trust in the democratic rules and the electoral system – the result being that the revolution is buried, with or without military honours.

Our aim here is not to draft a programme but to trace some paths, to suggest some examples, to propose some ideas for *creating the irreversible straight away*. Of these paths, many will be outlined in the landscape we know best: France. But the approach has nothing in common with what used to be known as 'socialism in one country'. The decay of democratic capitalism is such that, wherever the first shock occurs, its collapse will be international.

We must always bear in mind, however, the fear of chaos – quite a common feeling which, though ceaselessly boosted and exploited by the ideologues of domination, cannot for all that be treated with contempt. No one looks favourably on the prospect of being plunged into the dark with nothing to eat. If the huge rising force that points to a decisive break is to find and grasp the necessary lever, the first condition is to dispel the fear that exists in each and every one of us, to restore a relationship to the world rid of the anxieties of penury, deprivation and aggression that silently weave the tissue of *normal* existence. But, above all, it is necessary to distinguish the two fears that domination carefully amalgamates: fear of chaos and fear of the unknown. It is the moment of revolution – what it opens up, the joy that invariably accompanies it – which transforms the latter fear into an appetite for the unknown, into a thirst for the novel. Besides, one always underestimates the people's capacity to cope in exceptional situations.

In itself, a collapse of the apparatus of domination is never enough for the building of a new order. On the day following the victorious insurrection, it will be necessary to put in place barriers that prevent a return of the past, and to ensure that the ebb will not take the form of a 'return to normality'.

The state apparatus is in pieces, its debris whirling in empty space. Those who meet weekly to settle current business, and who are described against all the evidence as 'the government', are dazed and dotted around the natural landscape; some have taken flight. But with the first moments over, they will try to find one another again, to put their heads together, to prepare their revenge. If they are to remain harmless, they must be kept scattered. Such people operate through meetings, in offices, with files. We will take those away from them: we will close down, wall up and guard all the places where the wheels of the state were still turning yesterday – from the Elysée Palace to the most out-of-the-way subprefectures. Or we will turn them into crèches, hammams or popular canteens, as in the luxury hotels in Barcelona in 1936. We will cut their lines of communication, their intranets, their distribution lists, their secure telephone lines. If the fallen ministers and detested police chiefs want to meet in the back rooms of cafés, that's up to them. Without their offices, those officials will be incapable of action.

To take their vacated places, to sit in their empty armchairs and open their abandoned files, would be the worst of mistakes. We will not even think of doing that. Villages, local neighbourhoods and factories have places such as cinemas, schools, gyms or circuses, where it is possible to meet without having recourse to lecture halls that remind one of deadly general assemblies that just went on and on.

The dissolution of the constitutional bodies of the state, together with the dismissal of their personnel, will cut tens of thousands of people adrift. To those we should add the millions of 'unemployed', plus others whose professions will collapse or disappear: advertising staff, financiers, judges, police officers, soldiers, business school teachers – in short, a lot of people.

Let's stop speaking and thinking in terms of unemployment, jobs (gained or lost) and labour markets. Those despicable terms get us to see in human beings nothing more than their employability, to divide them into two classes (those with a job, who are fully alive, and all the rest, who are objectively and subjectively lesser). That centrality of employment – which is, in the vast majority of cases, *wage labour* – impels the education system to prepare young people for the concentrated horror of the 'corporate world'.

We can agree that work in the classical sense of the term – industrial or 'tertiary' – will not return. In fact, it would not have done so even if the insurrection had not taken place: no one can believe in the present incantations about reindustrialization, competitiveness, and so on. If there is one thing that will not be missed, it is indeed work as the founding myth that eats away at life: everyone will be glad to get rid of that, as they will of the pseudo-science of economics, which is indispensable to the smooth functioning of capitalism but is now about as useful as astrology.

A revolutionary situation is not only about the reorganization of society. It is also, and above all, the emergence of a new conception of life, a new tendency to joy. Work will not disappear just because its structures have collapsed; it will disappear out of a desire to experience collective activity differently.

What can and must be done on the day after the insurrection is to separate work and the means of existence, to abolish the individual necessity to 'earn one's living'. This has nothing to do with any 'social minimum thresholds', where the adjective 'social' applies, as in other cases, to every system of measurement intended to make people swallow the unacceptable. The point, rather, is that everyone should have their existence assured, not through paid employment that they are always in danger of losing or some other form of reduction to an individual lot, but through the very organization of collective life.

Of course, social relations being as they are for the moment, it is difficult to imagine the abolition of wage labour, or even an existence in which money is relegated to the margins. Is not money, in every area of life, the essential intermediary between our needs and their satisfaction? To get some idea of what a non-economic existence might be like, it is enough to look back at the insurrectionary moments of history, to remember what the Spanish insurgents of 1936 were saying, or the occupiers of Tahrir Square, or of the Odéon in Paris in May 1968. Those moments when nothing is work any longer but no one counts the efforts they make or the risks they take, when market relations have been shifted to the periphery of life, are also the moments of the highest individual and collective virtue. It will be objected that a world is not constructed on the basis of exceptional moments: that is certainly true, yet those moments indicate to us what needs to be done. From the first day after the insurrection, the break with the past order must be grounded upon the human pockets of resistance constituted in action, rather than the suppression of these because they are reluctant to obey orders. In contrast to the treatment that the Spanish Civil War reserved for columns of anarchist volunteers, or the French 'Liberation' for the Maquis, or the 'revolutionary organizations' for the action committees of 1968, one should not fear entrusting the essential tasks to groups of people already united by a non-economic mentality and the idea of a direct sharing of life as a whole. Those who have tasted that intoxication know what we mean to say, know the unforgettable flavour of that life. The abolition of economics cannot be decreed; it is built step by step.

The great peculiarity of our epoch with regard to the money question has not received much emphasis. Never has money been so ubiquitous, or so necessary for the least step we take in life, yet at the same time it has never been so dematerialized, so unreal. The fright caused by mere talk of the possibility of a bank run anywhere in the world (most recently in Cyprus) is enough for us to gauge the paradoxical vulnerability of that which forms the heart of present society. Money is no longer tangible matter, not even a scattered pile of bits of paper; it is no more than a sum of bits stored in secure computer networks. As far as bank accounts are concerned, it is possible to establish perfect equality through a few clicks on the central servers of a country's major banks.

However, there will be no repetition of the Bolshevik or Khmer Rouge mistake of abolishing money at the moment of the seizure of power.

The habit of falling back on one's isolated individuality when it comes to 'satisfying one's needs' – the habit of paying for everything in a world populated with potentially hostile strangers – will not disappear overnight. You cannot just step unscathed out of the world of economics. But fear of deprivation, general mistrust, compulsive accumulation for no purpose, copycat desires: everything that makes you a 'winner' in capitalist society will no longer be more than a grotesque defect in the new state of things.

What will remain of the centrality of money when we can eat our fill in one of the free canteens opened by various collectives on city boulevards, village squares and popular neighbourhoods, when we no longer have to pay rent to a landlord, when gas, electricity and water are no longer billed to each home but people are concerned to use and produce it as wisely and locally as possible, when books, theatres and cinemas are as free as 'peer to peer' music albums or films, when built-in obsolescence no longer forces us to buy a new mixer every six months and a new hi-fi system every three years? Perhaps money will continue to exist – if it is possible, as the inventors of bitcoin argue, to create a currency not resting upon a state order – but it will remain on the margins of both individual and collective existence. What shall we offer in return for the coffee of ex-Zapatistas from Chiapas or the chocolate of Senegalese communities, or the tea of Chinese comrades (much better than those we are used to from the toxic industrial plantations of capitalism)? Is there a kind of situation where the foreignness between human beings that characterizes market relations is appreciated as such, and therefore requires one or another form of currency? These are some of the questions that will demand reflection and experimentation.

One thing is certain, however: the need to own things diminishes insofar as they become simply and straightforwardly accessible. Instead of imagining a fixed sum of wealth to be shared in accordance with the well-known rules of the greatest greed, instead of adopting the bourgeois fantasy in which a whole council estate block comes to squat the apartments in a bourgeois neighbourhood of Paris, it would be better to think of what would happen if the brick-layers, roofers and decorators of the council estate were given the means to build in their own way, by following the wishes of the people living there. In a few years, as discussion among neighbours replaced the hypocritical code of planning permission, the council estate would become an architectural master-piece that people from all around the world would come to visit, as they already do the 'palace' built by the postman Ferdinand Cheval in Hauterives. Only the bourgeois think that everyone is envious of what they have. The whole attraction of what today's money can buy stems from the fact that it has been made inaccessible to nearly everyone, not from its being desirable in itself.

Let us deal here with a misguided 'good idea' that has been haunting liberal, and then left-ist, milieux for the past forty years: the idea of a guaranteed universal income or unconditional 'autonomy-expanding' benefit. Advocates of this 'realistic utopia', as they call it, never miss an opportunity to emphasize the *economic* feasibility of their 'revolution' here and now. Thus, for the disciples of Toni Negri, such an income, unconnected to work, would establish an unprecedented creativity within the new knowledge economy, which needs nothing else for each citizen to be as productive, and to live as well, as a Google employee. The costs and benefits have already been *calculated*, they say, and everything speaks in its favour: indeed, there is no longer any need for an insurrection or disorder to carry through such a revolution; it would be enough to introduce the guaranteed universal income, and we would all be spared the overhead costs of burned ministries, sacked police stations and injured cops. It would not even be necessary to break with capitalism: we would simply have to follow its logic to the end in order to arrive at communism, as everyone knows.

We could wear ourselves out arguing that such an income is unrealistic, that the countries that introduced it first would have to be police states capable of making an exact list of who lives in each dwelling. So here we have a measure that cannot be applied before the world dictatorship of the proletariat, which is not likely to happen at once. In fact, the guaranteed income claims to carry out the world revolution, which must already have taken place for that income to be possible. It maintains the very thing that the revolutionary process has to abolish: the centrality of money for existence, the individual character of income, the isolation of everyone with regard to their needs, the absence of life in common. The aim of the revolution is to shift money to the margins, to abolish economics; the trouble with the guaranteed income is that it preserves all the categories of economics.

We do not say that it would make no sense, in the emergency of the first few months after the insurrection, to pay everyone a certain sum levied from the accounts of the rich or the multinationals. That would allow time for life to be reorganized without the pressure of lack of money, in a period when there was a temporary lack of structures making it possible to live without money. What is more, we know that in terms of income the richest 10 per cent of households receive as much as the poorest 40 per cent, and that the inequality is even greater when it comes to inheritance. Such an order of magnitude means that an emergency transfer from the richest incomes to the poorest would enable everyone to survive in the first phase when everything is being turned upside down.

This way of looking at things runs counter to what is usually taught in the name of economics. Its oracles are regularly disproved, its sectaries, like the augurs of antiquity, cannot bump into one another without laughing, and what they preach about 'growth', 'development', 'competitiveness' or 'a way out of the crisis' can only express itself in poverty, distress and increased devastation. Nevertheless, economics has managed to impose itself everywhere as the science of needs, the science of reality, the *realistic* science par excellence. Even those who criticize capitalism often advance the project of a 'different economics'; there is currently a manifesto in the bookshops that speaks of 'changing economics'. They think that, beneath the capitalist misuse, there lies hidden a more or less natural system of needs that might be satisfied by assigning a human purpose to the existing means of production, by placing them *at the service of all*. They think that somewhere there is a 'real economy', to be saved from the tentacles of finance. It is one of the merits of the recent 'horse-meat' scandal to have shown everyone that finance does not hover above a healthy, artisanal economy but forms its ordinary, daily core.

One has only to read Xenophon's *Economics* to understand what the subject is about. That dialogue concerns the best way for a master to run his domain. What should he do to ensure that his slaves work as well as possible and produce the most wealth under the iron rule of his wife–steward? Or that his wife manages the slaves with the greatest diligence and efficiency? Or that the master has to spend the least time in his *oikos*, and that his domain procures him the greatest material power and wealth? How should he organize the economic subjugation of the household in order to control as well as possible the servitude of his people?

Note in passing that the term 'control' derives etymologically from medieval bookkeeping techniques, which checked every calculation on a '*contre*-rouleau', a counter-scroll. When political economy was born, in the seventeenth century, it showed straight away a concern to ensure that the 'free activity' of the subjects should ensure the maximum of material power for the sovereign. As the science of the wealth of sovereigns and then of nations, economics is thus essentially the science of slave control, the science of subjugation. This is why its main tool is measurement, with market value as only a means to that end. It is necessary to measure in order to control, because the master must be able to devote himself entirely to politics. From its origins, economics organized servitude in such a way that the production of slaves was measurable. If Fordism became universal for a time, it was because it enabled the capitalist not only to produce more but to measure the workers' activity in minute detail. The extension of economics is in this sense identical with the extension of the measurable, which is itself identical with the extension of capitalism. Those who expose the near-universal spread of evaluative techniques into the least suspected corners of human conduct testify to the penetration of capitalism into our lives, our bodies, our souls.

Economics does indeed deal with needs: that is, the needs of the dominators, their need for control. There is not a real economy that is a victim of finance capital; there is only one mode of *political* organization of servitude. Its hold over the world comes from its capacity to measure everything, thanks to the global diffusion of all kinds of digital devices – computers, sensors, iPhones, etc. – which are directly systems of control.

The abolition of capitalism is above all the abolition of economics, the end of measurement, or the imperialism of measurement. At the moment, it is necessary to measure for the one who is not there, for the master, for the central brain or office, in order that the one who is not there has a hold on the one who is there (this is known soberly as 'reporting'). Those who live there, who work there, are well aware of what they need to measure for their own local organization: the man who heats his home with wood has an interest in measuring the number of cubic metres he has in his garage; those who produce such and such a machine have an interest in measuring the stocks of metal they have before they launch into production. As for the forms of production whose only virtue is to be controllable from afar, by the boss or head office, they will be destroyed and give way to a different rationality from *that of the master*.

To refuse to make work the linchpin of existence is to fly in the face of common sense. The response is not long in coming: if everyone can choose to live without working, no one will work any more – a disaster. But for what? For whom? In the movement that brings yoghurt into a refrigerator, there must first of all be cows and a dairy, but there must *also* be hundreds of people to design the pot and packaging, to find the colouring, to check the taste, to launch the TV advertising; there must be technicians, people to print the packaging, to stick posters to publicity hoardings, and people who transport the pots of yoghurt, put them in the right place on supermarket shelves, stop anyone from trying to steal them; there must be cashiers and manufacturers of cash registers. Let us turn the facts around: the world of yoghurt pots does not make thousands of people live; it forces them into meaningless lives. Hundreds of thousands of hours will be set free when we have large dairies from which pots leave without a label and without colouring. Once the world of capital unravels,

59

the yoghurt will be better and a thousand times less time-consuming for the human community.

The common-sense argument ('those who do not work do not eat') is wrong for at least three reasons:

I. A lot of people who work today get up in the morning without difficulty, either because their work interests them or because friendship and team spirit give them enough satisfaction. But most of them are wage earners, conscious of selling their labour power to create wealth that goes into pockets other than their own. Then there are the various miseries of the wage-earning condition: the weight of the hier-archy, the obsession with productivity, the various forms of harassment, the fear of losing one's job. If, despite everything, some wage earners now already get pleasure from their work, what will they not feel once it is no longer imposed on them by the need to 'earn a living', once they are able to choose it freely? And when building workers will work to house their brothers and sisters, and no longer to enrich the shareholders of the multinationals, the atmosphere on building sites will doubtless be quite different.

2. With the end of democratic capitalism, the total quantity of work will decline. *Necessary* work will continue to diminish, as it has done continually since the end of Fordism and since the electronic revolution (a phenomenon linked, of course, with the shift of production to the Asian industrial infernos, although there too cracks are clearly audible). Most important, we shall see the disappearance of a huge mass of work *that has no purpose* other than to display publicly the *servitude imperative*. Democratic capitalism has created millions of jobs in the world that serve to establish operational and certificatory norms and to assess their application. In the so-called public sector as well as the private, experts daily invent new procedures and set new targets and indicators, putting to work crowds of auditors, bookkeepers, inspectors, mathematicians and

'reporting' specialists. The dismantling of this global office, which is indispensable for the abstract and largely fictitious operation of democratic capitalism, will induce a sharp fall in the number of 'workstations'. But what was considered a disaster in the age of compulsory work – the job losses regularly deplored by ministers on an ad hoc basis – will bring great flexibility in the choice between work and non-work: there will be more than enough workers, released by the meltdown of the bureaucratic society of guided consumption, to ensure the production of really necessary goods.

3. It is true that there will always be unpleasant work that involves getting dirty or is simply boring. In the West, this is at present assigned to human groups for whom the white Christian masses have the least consideration – the most recent arrivals or those with the darkest skins. To share it around more generally is to fight against both segregation and another malady: the division of labour. Theorized by Plato, analysed

by Marx, this runs deeper today than ever. It is said that Louis XIV courteously greeted the women who came to clean the parquet floors of Versailles and make them glisten. Nowadays a top executive never meets his cleaning personnel, who are indeed not part of his company. In his L-shaped daily itinerary – the horizontal stretch being from his villa in a wealthy suburb to the parking lot in his high-rise block, the vertical trunk being the elevator from the ground floor to his office – the only manual worker he comes close to is his chauffeur. Immaterial (not to say 'intellectual') labour and manual labour inhabit two different planets.

To divide up necessary but unrewarding tasks among everyone cannot be done successfully in authoritarian fashion; the attempts in this direction during the Chinese Cultural Revolution were more like re-education camps for intellectuals, which have not left behind good memories. To gain acceptance for a fair distribution of tasks is a matter of scale. If I have chosen to continue my profession as a dermatologist or book dealer, and if there is a need in my street or the next for a postal worker, a sweeper or a butcher's assistant, I will learn one or another of these new jobs and willingly spend two or three afternoons a week on them – willingly, because in my neighbourhood or district everyone will freely accept them as necessary and meaningful. Neighbours will become workmates and, in some cases, friends. A dustcart team can be a happy, tightly knit team if it consists of volunteers who will perhaps be doing something different the next month. An attachment to colleagues, which can be seen every day in the mournful enterprises of capitalism, has the power to overshadow the unpleasant nature of a job.

The end of compulsory work, the end of the dictatorship of economics, will almost automatically entail the end of the state. On this point, one runs up against 'common sense' once more, but not only common sense: most revolutionaries have always doubted that it is possible to do without the state as a central organization of constraint – and this has led most revolutions to act against their own cause by turning the revolution into an intensified form of state subjugation. At work here is an old anthropological belief going back to Saint Augustine or, if you like, Thucydides. According to this, 'man' is a fallen, evil creature, inclined to give free rein to his most brutal, most anti-social passions and spurred on by the most guilty and destructive desires; or, to put it in the neutral language of economics, he tends to 'pursue his own interests'. This means that man is essentially no more than a tyrant, driven by his needs and by blind nature. Hobbes, whom Marx described as 'the greatest economist of all time', gave canonical formulation to this belief and drew the most rigorous consequences: since man is essentially bad, a social contract is needed to establish a state that will put an end to 'the war of all against all'. It is a secularized theological argument, which has since become a kind of commonplace *wherever there is a state*. The more one seeks to establish an authoritarian state, the more one exaggerates this founding thesis: a young neo-Nazi, for example, writing recently in *La France orange mécanique* under the pen name Laurent Obertone, put forward the idea of a 'nation turned savage' to gain an audience for his fantasies of a restored Pétainist state. Conversely, the gentle Prince Kropotkin tried to show, in his *Mutual Aid: A Factor of Evolution*, that nature is dominated not by 'the struggle for existence' but by cooperation: and therefore that the human species can live without the state.

When a revolution breaks out, all this metaphysics of 'man' and bazaar anthropology comes crashing down. During the Paris Commune, Gustave Courbet wondered at how simply, and how impeccably, everything organized itself without a central authority. The same amazement was apparent among the people themselves during the Spanish Civil War; the same incredulity among Tunisian and Egyptian intellectuals at the grandeur of a population suddenly transformed in their being by the revolution. Yesterday a subdued, narrow-minded people of slaves, today proud, noble, courageous beings, their feelings stripped of pettiness. This does not prove that man is good, any more than the existence of cannibalistic violators of children proves that man is a wolf to man. There is simply no such thing as 'man'. If there is anything that really produces a vile, abject, wretched, deceitful being, then it is state constraint.

We have to give up all political anthropology. If the state is in no way necessary, this is not because man is good but because 'man' is a subject mass-produced by the state and its anthropology. There are only ways of being, organizing, speaking to one another, historical moments, languages and embodied beliefs. Only by organizing freely together with those around us can we try out forms of existence in which the virtues of each person find expression, and flaws, cracks and weaknesses can be mitigated.

There is a simple answer to those who ask how a country can survive the disappearance of the state apparatus: *that apparatus serves no purpose*, or, more precisely, it serves no other purpose than its own reproduction. That is the central preoccupation, as we can see from the energy with which every newly elected public figure, from the president of the United States to the mayor of a rural commune, immediately starts working for his own re-election.

However, the activity of the state apparatus has a number of significant side effects, the first of which is to keep the people out of decisions concerning it. When the French and Dutch in 2005, or the Irish in 2008, rejected the draft EU constitution drawn up in Brussels, it was explained to them that they had misunderstood the proposal and a way round their refusal was soon found. In October 2011, when it was a question of asking Greeks what they thought of a partial debt writedown at the price of the 'troika' grip on their country, pressure from the G-20 and rumours of a coup d'état led to the sudden abandonment of the referendum. The elementary forms of 'representative democracy' are no longer respected anywhere: men and women elected at the polls are allowed to participate only in secondary debates;

the real decisions are taken behind the scenes by 'the markets', and by the international organizations and teams of experts.

We sometimes hear talk of a 'conflict of interests' – for instance, when a minister or elected local politician sells off part of the public domain at a knockdown price to a company with which he is on friendly terms. In fact, the expression is not well chosen: the correct one is 'common interests'. In France, the big property developers, aircraft manufacturers and arms dealers, who own all the national press, have exactly the same interests as the 'decision makers' in any democratic capitalist government. Indeed, the individuals are often the same: they can be seen moving to and fro between the so-called public sector and the multinational corporations where 'the markets' invest. If there is a trial now and then, or if the media put on a show of indignation over some particularly flagrant case, it is no more than a safety valve necessary in a country where there is still freedom of opinion.

'A people has only one dangerous enemy: its government. Yours has constantly waged war on you with impunity' (Saint-Just, *Report on Government*, 10 October 1793).

To create the irreversible, the reconstitution of a state must be avoided. Orthodox Marxists will evoke the 'withering away of the state' and quote Lenin's *State and Revolution*, but the history of the West shows that states born of a revolution have never allowed themselves to wither away. On the contrary, all have worked to strengthen their apparatus, and that strengthening has always involved *the elimination of the far left*, of the marching wing of the revolution. From Thomas Münzer's rebellious peasantry to the workers of the Shanghai Commune, from the Levellers of the English Civil War to the Cordeliers Club in Year Two of the French Republic, from the insurgents of Kronstadt and Ukraine to the Spanish anarchists and POUMists, all have suffered a tragic end. There is something strange about this repetition in such different eras and circumstances. One possible explanation: a state born of a revolution clashes with the forces it has driven out, with an internal counter-revolution supported or not from abroad; organization, order and centralism are needed to confront it; but the far left tends instead to deepen the revolution, to go beyond purely political emancipation, to change the very forms of life. Its efforts inevitably sow disorder, so that from being attractive it soon becomes intolerable to those who are trying to run the apparatus of the new state. The inevitable showdown then takes place at the expense of the poorly armed and organized, the passionate but sometimes confused spirits to be found on the far left.

For our part, then, we shall not fear disorder; we shall accept divergences, rather than flee from conflicts that make us stronger. We shall transform 'politics' into a huge field of collective experiments, avoiding the formation of frustrated blocs that are unable to get their voices heard.

Those who believe in a collective human nature think that the French system is tainted with Jacobinism. We need not dwell on the historical absurdity of this: although there really were Jacobins, 'Jacobinism' is no more than an old calumny spread around by the Thermidorean reaction. In particular, the term masks the essential dysfunctionality – which is that most of the questions at issue are neither raised nor dealt with where they should be, at the right level. Bureaucratic centralism is everywhere rampant, and it is scarcely less formidable than the democratic centralism dear to the old 'communist' parties. For example, any non-nuclear electrician knows how absurd is the dogma of the centralized production of electricity. From a straightforwardly economic point of view, what is lost in high-tension lines stretching over hundreds of kilometres and what is spent in running huge power stations represents a cost which, if taken into account, should lead to their being dropped overnight. In terms of vulnerability – breakdowns or other incidents – it is precisely the centralization of production that poses the greatest danger. A set of local production networks, interconnected at a number of points, is the best way of guarding against the risk of collapse that is supposed to justify constant improvement of the existing system.

Similarly, it is bureaucratic centralism – ministerial programmes – which compels all school-children in France to learn history and geography in the same way, irrespective of the region in which they live. And it is bureaucratic centralism which ensures the strict application of competition laws, with the result that people in Provence are fed on Dutch tomatoes and fish from African lakes.

It may be objected that the purpose of French decentralization has been to avoid just such phenomena. Designed and introduced by Gaston Defferre, one of the most authoritarian wheeler-dealers in the Socialist Party hierarchy during the Mitterrand years, this policy functioned like a cluster bomb, scattering endless new authorities in which bureaucratic centralism remained alive and kicking.

More recently, a reform of the 'community of local communes' has been under way, with the official aim of achieving economies of scale, but with the actual result that smaller communes deemed too autonomous are placed under the thumb of an urban centre. This is the schema of the metropolis in miniature, which reproduces the old colonial system at the level of the region. As the small commune is the last instance where the popular will sometimes expresses itself, the intention is to whittle down its capacities. By eliminating a school here (in favour of bussing all over the area) and a job there, by causing the café and the baker's shop to disappear, the programme actually destroys the most appropriate scale in the name of economies that profit no one very obvious.

While it is not possible to change the material organization of a country from one day to the next, the scale of the organization of human communities can be changed almost immediately. The irreversible aspect here is to restore the control that human beings have lost over their immediate conditions of existence. The point is not to take over, even collectively, the set of infrastructures that materialize the loss of human control – from superstores through nuclear power stations to television channels and mobile phone networks. It is at the level of the village and the neighbourhood, or anyway at a *local* level, that a new, collective manner of matching needs and the means of satisfying them will be able to emerge. In fact, that will do no more than link up with historical forms of organization, from the Parisian *sections* of 1793 to the *quilombos* of Brazil.

In the various assemblies, work groups, collectives and committees, the main thing to avoid is formalism – the idea that decision making must follow a standard procedure modelled on parliament. In March 1871, the unelected Central Committee of the National Guard – a 'gathering of obscure figures', according to the historian Lissagaray, which lacked formal legitimacy – organized the seizure of power by the people, put reaction to flight, and took over the running of public services. Everything changed when this committee made way for the General Council of the Commune. Regularly elected by the twenty arrondissements of Paris, this body proved incapable of organizing the resistance and wasted time on sterile discussions between its authoritarian majority and a more or less libertarian minority – an exemplary case of the ravages of parliamentarism in a time of revolution.

Another decision-making authority is the general assembly, subject in principle to the rules of 'direct democracy'. Here too, the variety of situations, customs, links and forms of expression is drastically curtailed by the procedural uniformity – hence the dire quality and crushing boredom so palpable in general assemblies as well as in the internal meetings of small political groups. The ones who get their way are those with the greatest endurance; they alone, the 'creatures of power', are able to tolerate such massive doses of gloom and fatigue, since they are themselves already filled with lethal doses of bitterness.

That leaves the cases where, despite every effort, two irreconcilable positions confront each other. This means that there has to be a vote, which represents a *failure to agree*. So as not to compound this with the shame of secrecy, people will register their vote by standing up or remaining seated, or by some other open method, as in the Parisian *sections* of Year Two. The clearest example of what has to be avoided is the kind of secret vote that brings a strike to an end, after a general meeting called by the trade unions or the company bosses or often both. 'Leave the darkness and the secret ballot to criminals and slaves: free men wish to have the people as witness to their thoughts' (Robespierre, *Speech on the Constitution*, 10 May 1793).

In what is commonly known as the enterprise, the utterly opaque forms of decision making that exist today will disappear along with the bosses. It is no longer possible to think that the revolution will consist simply of taking the means of production into common ownership; there was certainly 'collective appropriation' under 'actually existing socialism', and we saw the results. Besides, in Spain, Greece and Portugal, the revolt against the ongoing devastation does not spontaneously take the form of workers' councils – in factories that are vanishing before people's eyes – but rather of an unexpected renewal of the cooperative movement. This is leading to the strange idea of the *integral cooperative*, where not only production but the whole of life is organized.

One idea doing the rounds is that the internet and 'social networks' make it possible to revive the famous direct democracy of the Greek agora, where all the citizens met to take decisions. You get the idea: direct democracy can arise only in small-sized human groups, but electronic link-ups that eliminate distances make the whole world a potential agora.

In reality, the exact opposite is true. The designation of sterile, exhibitionist networks as 'social' speaks volumes about what society in the West has become. (A new adjective, 'societal', has even been created to mark the quasi-feudal escheat of 'the social'.) If posters in the Paris Metro offer contacts for a fee, if every passenger taps pointless messages and listens to canned music, it is because of the need to ward off feelings of isolation in the crowd *without people having to speak to one another*. The result is not consciously pursued, but it is in the logic of the market: what is free today will bring in billions tomorrow. That was not the case with the black and white balls that the citizens of Athens used to indicate their decisions.

Of course the internet is the quickest way to communicate in emergency situations. It was decisive in bringing down the corrupt regimes in Tunisia and Egypt, and no doubt it will be decisive too in the coming insurrection. It enables people to get round the monopoly of information held by the state and private media. But as for its 'democratic' role, a system in which you don't know who is speaking and opinions are inconsequential for those who express them – in short, a system where you can spread literally anything around – will not replace eye and hand contact, a shared drink, enthusiasm and argument, the real 'social relations' that belong to the realm of friendship rather than sociology.

After the break-up of the state apparatus, the main task will be to divide up the affairs of the collective at the most appropriate level. For those pertaining to the local area – housing, food, schools, transport, enterprises, etc. – the new ideas will emerge in the neighbourhoods and reconstituted communes. It would be absurd to handle such matters in the same way everywhere. In France, for example, what is common to problems of schooling in Lozère and Seine-Saint-Denis, or Mayenne and the Marseilles conurbation? Bureaucratic centralism, with its succession of contradictory ministerial directives, has caused havoc here, and it will be necessary to carry out modest ad hoc improvements, through trial and error and collective interventions.

But some fields will have to be addressed at the higher level of the province (the 'region', a bureaucratic entity, will have disappeared) or the country as a whole. The dismantling of the nuclear industry and its repercussions for the general supply of energy; the fate of the major highways and air, river and rail transport; the orientation to be given to the motor industries and others; the ways in which the national information media should be given back to the people: these are a few examples of questions that cannot be answered locally.

It is often easy to draw the dividing line between what can be resolved here and now and what pertains to a higher level. With regard to public health, for instance, the siting of dispensaries, emergency services and specialist hospital facilities, or non-authoritarian ways of feeding practitioners into 'medical deserts' and addressing any shortage of nurses, anaesthetists and midwives, are clearly local issues. They were impossible to solve under democratic capitalism, because it was said that the necessary funds were not available. But everything will change as soon as health has ceased to be a major focus of profit-making and the running of things is entrusted to those who have chosen to work there. This is not a naïve fantasy. After the Cuban revolution, medicine in that country became the best in Latin America and infant mortality fell to the level of the industrial countries – all without any noteworthy injection of cash.

Let us go further. If the hospital is no longer considered an enterprise, if it is returned to its original purpose as a tool for the community, really major changes are perfectly conceivable. It will be possible to get rid of various parasitic jobs in specialized budgeting, the checking of standards, and the monitoring of profitability. Medical and nursing personnel will be relieved of the administrative tasks that have weighed on them for the past twenty years. Management will be in the hands of a small team of doctors and nurses that is renewed once a year – a part of the hospital staff previously confined to subaltern roles, but which knows better than anyone what needs to be done to provide the best care. The hospital will fight against the division of labour, by involving all the staff in 'non-noble' tasks such as cleaning, sterilization and the wheeling around of patients, and by making it easier for individuals to develop their careers and to move from caring to medical jobs. This cultural revolution will take place with the support of the local population, which will be pleasantly surprised to find itself welcomed through the doors and not shunted into despairing queues. One might even hope that the hospital will one day cease to be the fortified place where the populace is medicalized, that it will spread around it the delicate art of identifying pain and treating one's own and other people's ailments: the *caring mission* it has monopolized for so long.

But today, wherever democratic capitalism holds sway, public health is being eaten away by a kind of cancer that cannot be treated locally: that is, the pharmaceutical and medical imaging industries, two of the most prosperous and aggressive on the international scene. Together, they combine to dig the famous 'social security hole', which serves as an argument to justify the deterioration of medicine for the poor.

To expropriate, nationalize or transform into workers' cooperatives the branches of the great German, Swiss or American drug companies is a necessary but insufficient minimum. Their whole output needs to be monitored, in order to eliminate the thousands of useless drugs that mendacious publicity, foisted on GPs by travelling salesmen in medical guise, causes us to swallow throughout the year. It is a specialized task to sift through this vast display and select what is worth keeping, to determine and divide up the main lines of research; moreover, it will be necessary to choose carefully the men and women for the job, bearing in mind the errant ways of the 'drug agencies', which are all contaminated by their incestuous contacts with the pharmaceutical industry.

The difficulty is perhaps even greater when it comes to medical imaging, since a number of magical beliefs have to be confronted and dispelled. By placing their spectacular images in medical journals and the general press, the international corporations that produce ultrasound, MRI (magnetic resonance imaging) and other types of scanner have managed to spread the idea that cross sections of the human body, if sufficiently precise and targeted, will necessarily show the origins of what is wrong. This myth has two consequences. On the one hand, it allows thousands of hugely expensive devices to be sold around the world, which then have to be kept going to make them pay; hence the large component of (mostly pointless) imaging in the 'social security hole'. (In France, radiologists – the name for those who have bought such devices and employ low-paid, low-status 'operators' to handle them – are at the top of the medical income scale.) On the other hand, the magic of imagery distracts from good medicine, most of which is practised with words, eyes, hands and a few simple tools. Without rejecting progress, we might underline what should be evident enough: that it is both effective and cost-free to register what the patient complains of, to examine the troubled knee, to palpate the spleen, to listen to the lungs, and so on. But these actions take more time and demand more attention than the ordering of a scan – which is what the patient asks for, so powerful is the imagers' marketing. It is necessary to spread a whole new conception of medicine, among both doctors and patients, since the apparatuses will remain in place for many years once the industrial lobbies have been made powerless to do harm.

These tendencies in public health will doubtless reappear elsewhere, in food and agriculture as well as scientific research. To create the irreversible, it is at local level that new ideas will see the light of day and unexpected solutions will be invented. The main task at higher levels will be to erase the after-effects of the old world.

The local invention and differential implementation of new lifestyles is a conception that goes against the abstract unity of the republic deeply rooted in people's thinking in a country like France. The republican school, republican values, a single law for the whole national territory: French men and women hold these notions dear and attach them more or less consciously to the memory of the Revolution. But what has been forgotten, and what history teachers are careful not to recall, is that the centralism of the Revolution was a necessity linked to the circumstances of the time. In its origins, the revolutionary movement sought to destroy the pyramidal system of the absolutist monarchy. There was *no representative of the central power* in the *départements* of France at the moment of their creation. In the big cities – Paris, but also Marseilles and Lyons – the *sections* invented their own operational rules and ceaselessly displayed their will to be autonomous. The republic, 'one and indivisible', was no more than a way of affirming revolutionary cohesion in a country torn by civil war and threatened with break-up in the form of Girondin 'federalism'. It was war, both civil and external, that led to the formation of a *revolutionary government* (a contradiction in terms often noted at the time), which reined in the popular movement and established a centralism that has lasted ever since, in forms more or less authoritarian according to the conjuncture.

To put an end to that centralism, we should not listen to the voices of 'the Left': we should refuse to bow to the scarecrow that is today's republic, with its frills appended in the aftermath of the Commune by the grim Third Republic and widely utilized in its colonial enterprise: the tricolour flag, the secular principle, the Marseillaise (which blacks and Arabs in France's football team have every reason not to sing) and the mafia-like 'republican discipline' in the second round of electoral contests.

Another scarecrow is communitarianism, which the Right fields to justify 'the rule of law' and the deployment of the police on every occasion to ensure respect for it. Evidently it is intolerable to the republic that segregated and harassed young people have created their own linguistic, musical and sartorial codes, or that they use religion to assert themselves in the face of those who treat them with contempt. Against them is unleashed the ferocity of the crime squads and of intellectuals attached to good manners and the correct use of the subjunctive. But those young people will play their role in the toppling of democratic capitalism. They will apply the politics of the tower block entrance halls, which is worth as much as that of France Culture broadcasts and editorials in a servile press.

The issues that concern the country as a whole bristle with difficulties that have never and nowhere been properly resolved. They revolve around what classical philosophers used to call *representation of the people* and expression of *the general will.*

The idea handed down from the past, which naturally comes to mind on the day after a victorious insurrection, is to elect an assembly while endeavouring to avoid the pitfalls of classical parliamentarism: that is, to insist on a binding mandate with a time limit, on the possibility of recalling representatives, and so on. But whatever the precautions, such an assembly will more or less correspond to the country as it was on the eve of the meltdown of democratic capitalism. The most illustrious assembly in French history, the Convention Nationale, had a majority of Physiocrats (we would say liberals) raised in the school of Turgot and Quesnay. When Thermidor arrived and the iron grip of the most determined revolutionaries had been broken, the centrist-liberal 'swamp' they had previously managed to carry along with them took power in the assembly and, in keeping with its true nature, went over to the side of reaction and economic liberalism.

On the other hand, it is hard to see how an elected assembly could deal in an informed manner with such diverse fields as photovoltaics, river transport and the elimination of pesticides. It might be said that this is the case today, but that is precisely the point. For decades now (in fact, always) national assemblies have not solved anything – because parliamentarians do not know the subjects at issue, because they are often in thrall to contradictory interests and pressures, and because the very workings of a parliament do not allow serious debate. The allocation of work to specialist commissions is only a pretence, since each one is a mini-parliament, whose members seek only to assert their own image and that of their party.

And how could an assembly do without an executive? To return to the Convention during the French Revolution, it is true that ministers were reduced to the role of docile implementers of decisions, but the Committee of Public Safety – a creature of the legislature, elected by the assembly and in principle renewed each month – was a de facto executive. Once an executive system has been created, its natural tendency will be towards efficiency – how could it be blamed for that? – and therefore to greater centralization. In this way the circle will be closed. Starting from the way it exists today, bureaucratic centralism will have been first destroyed and then reconstituted with different names, different administrative grades and different uniforms. Until now, all revolutions have followed this pattern – except for those like the Paris Commune which did not have enough time.

If we are to avoid parliamentarism, history serves only to assist reflection on past failures. The solutions have to be invented.

It might be laid down, for instance, that each issue for which the most appropriate level of decision making is national should be handled by a working group based in a different town, the former capital being only one of the possibilities. Such fragmentation is easy to imagine in countries like Germany, Italy or the United States, which are not built around a single city. It is more problematic, but even more important, in France, where Paris still serves as a base camp for the centralism of the 'indivisible republic'. The ephemeral communes set up in March 1871 in a number of working-class towns (Lyons, Saint-Étienne, Le Creusot, Marseilles), with the idea that the country should function on the model of a commune, left only a rather faint trace in the collective memory. This time, geographical fragmentation will be facilitated if, as is probable, Paris has not been the epicentre of the revolution. If the implosion of democratic capitalism begins in Toulouse, Amiens or Vaulx-en-Velin, and if the movement spreads to the Paris region in the same way as to the rest of France, it will be all the easier to dissolve the traditional revolutionary centralism.

What name should be given to these working groups set up around the country? The question may appear secondary, but let us remember that in January 1967, when revolutionaries adopted the name Shanghai Commune after they had deposed the local party bosses and taken power in the city, their choice was accepted by Beijing for only a few weeks. After that, out of fear that communes would spread to the whole of China – and thus put an end to the centralized party – the name changed to Shanghai Revolutionary Committee, marking the beginning of the end of that singular experience.

It would take us out of our present line of argument to set a number for the working groups or to specify the distribution of tasks among them. But one can imagine how they will be formed. The election of representatives would turn them into mini-parliaments, with all the drawbacks we have seen. Another procedure, however, would be to include people *who wish to take part in them*: who are interested in the question, who have thought about it and who have, or have had, a job in the sector – in short, volunteers. There is little risk that people will push and shove to join such groups out of opportunism or the lure of material advantage, since the role will not bring financial benefits but rather a sacrifice of time and energy that shakes up daily life. This is one of the reasons why it will be of short duration, with others taking over by roster.

Each working group will have a coordinator, not a fixed chairperson, responsible for the material organization, recording and broadcasting of meetings, and so on. For difficult issues, it might invite scientific or technical specialists, who will have nothing in common with the experts of old; they will be chosen from supporters of the new course and will take part in discussions on an equal footing with everyone else. For example, the committee in charge of dismantling the nuclear industry might include power station workers, people living nearby, members of anti-nuclear groups, and physicists, engineers and technicians in the electricity and wider energy sector, without anyone being able to use the argument from authority.

As for its 'decisions', the best way of ensuring that they remain sensible is not 'popular control' (which is always open to manipulation) but a clear mode of application. In the absence of a central executive, it will be up to the working groups themselves to implement the measures they propose. Direct confrontation with the practical implications of a measure, as well as a duty to convince the general public, will deter people from suggesting unachievable solutions or ones dictated by some unavowed interest.

A system so contrary to the habits inherited from Colbert, the French Revolution and republican practices cannot function without hitches. A degree of disorder will have to be accepted for a time, as the consequence of a choice not to have the revolution led by the centre or by an uncontrollable, irremovable political party doomed to bureaucratic senescence. In fact, many political systems have been born amid disorder. Even American democracy, commonly presented as a model of peaceful evolution, came about in a context of violence, in which the struggle for independence went together with an undercover war of the poor against the rich. 'In the first half of the 19th century, what fascinated outsiders was the sheer implausibility [of democracy in America]. Could you really do politics like this, with such fractured and chaotic popular input? It seemed unlikely anything so ramshackle could last long' (David Runciman, *London Review of Books*, 21 March 2013).

Democratic capitalism works assiduously to destroy the planet. (Barracks communism too proved how efficient it could be by drying up the Aral Sea through cotton monoculture, and by developing the Trabant with its backfiring exhaust of black smoke that transformed cities like Leipzig and Magdeburg into soot-covered phantoms.) The process cannot simply be expected to come to an end with the disappearance of the system that set it in train. One of the preconditions will be to get rid of the 'ecology' disaster once and for all. Today it operates as an opium of the people, by adding an indispensable dose of morality to modern marketing ('green' cars, biological washing powder, organic chickens). It seeks to make us feel guilty *on behalf of our children*, on the grounds that, being unable to meet the criteria laid down at various 'earth summits', we will bequeath to them global warming in addition to high levels of debt and unsustainable pensions. Like any religion, ecology also tries to sow fear with events, non-events or straightforward lies whipped up by docile media: the acid rain that was supposed to be destroying all the forests of eastern Europe (how many years have gone by since that was last talked about?); the hole in the ozone layer (which seems to be closing up again), and epidemics likely to kill a large part of the human species (Creutzfeldt-Jakob syndrome or 'mad cow' disease, strains of bird flu that can be passed on to humans, the H1N1 flu virus, coronaviruses, etc.).

We have no wish to deny the terrible environmental degradation suffered by the Inuit or by the indigenous peoples of the Amazon, the general disturbance of the world's climate, but let us have no more of the ecologists' patter that is drummed into schoolchildren from an early age and serves to fuel political pseudo-debates. (In France, this reached a peak in the French presidential election campaign of 2007, when the main candidates swore allegiance in the presence of a former TV host and ecological guru, who has since become the 'special envoy of the president of the republic for the protection of nature'.)

Sorting and recycling are tiny gestures of exorcism in comparison with the scale of the disaster caused by democratic capitalism and the variants of market economy current in the new industrial countries. What is mainly fuelling the capitalist apparatus of global destruction is the proliferation of cities, whose ravages pile up from day to day by virtue of a twofold mechanism. On the one hand, the process of concentration inherited from the nineteenth century and twentieth-century Fordism created a number of industrial centres, some of which are now ruined (Manchester, Detroit, Marseilles), but which overall still attract a profusion of job-seekers. The 'information revolution' absorbs only a tiny fraction of these, so that most join the ranks of the unemployed and zero-security workers, while the metropolitan areas themselves continue their anarchic growth in a game of smoke and mirrors.

On the other hand, capitalism has turned the world of the countryside upside down. 'Modern' agriculture does not need a peasantry for its conversion of land into a chemical substratum, or for its machinery resembling army tanks (and it is a war that is being waged against bad weeds, bad nature and bad insects, with collateral damage for the birds and the bees). In nearly all the poor countries, the subsistence agriculture that keeps people fed is being driven out by the industrial monoculture *necessary* for the growth of cities.

The destructive effect of mega-cities derives not only from their waste products, their exhaust gases and their useless consumption of all kinds of energy. Not the least of their ills is the way in which they spread like tumours. The phenomenon has been around for a long time and is well known in poor countries. Shanty towns, favelas, plank-and-cardboard villages are part of the scenery around big cities – from India to Brazil, from Nigeria to Malaysia. In 'developed' countries, the poor were expelled from city centres a long time ago, but now their exile is driving them beyond outlying districts towards areas even more ramshackle and inhospitable than the inner suburbs. On what used to be farmland, one no longer finds even the semblance of a centre around a church or town hall. To feed themselves, pensioners and poverty-stricken families, many of them recent immigrants, have to travel long distances to the nearest supermarket: local agriculture is no more than a memory. In France, the struggle of Nantes farmers against the airport at Notre-Dame-des-Landes, or of inhabitants of the Susa valley against the Lyons–Turin high-speed railway line, are the media-highlighted tip of a huge iceberg. French ministerial statistics show that 160 hectares of arable land are destroyed every day by the proliferation of cities, while on another scale altogether the Chinese megalopolises are growing so fast that they transform tens of millions of uprooted peasants into impoverished migrants.

At the same time, life is gradually being extinguished in numerous European villages. The

most beautiful and best-situated are kept alive arti-
ficially by tourism and the transformation of old
stones into second homes.

In France, the post-1968 movement back to
the land – goat rearing plus collective farms – has left
few traces outside the Cévennes, Ariège and Ardèche.
Nowadays, the poor rarely leave the city to set themselves up in the countryside – not because they are
attached to their urban or peri-urban setting, but
because *there is no work elsewhere.* It's better to remain
a temporary security guard or to clean metro trains,
better to spend four hours a day commuting, than to
starve to death.

The end of the centrality of work, the delink-
ing of job and livelihood, will change everything. The
poor and the less poor will leave their dilapidated
shanties and mobile homes, bring abandoned villages
back to life, reopen cafés and baker's shops; their presence will relieve the boredom of old people who have
stayed put while waiting to die. And for those who
wish it, there will be no lack of building sites.

Sceptics might like to ponder two exemplary cases. The first concerns the Plateau de Millevaches in the Limousin region of France, which various groups have set out to repopulate in the past ten years, organizing in such a way as to opt out of the economy and to make themselves materially and politically more autonomous. Some of them settled in the now famous village of Tarnac, where they were well received by a mayor, Georges Guingouin, from the revolutionary communist tradition. Together they coped with the tasks of building and farm work, and engaged in political intervention and reflection. In November 2008, however, the regime of the day – Michèle Alliot-Marie, the interior minister, egged on by the eminent criminologist Professor Alain Bauer – tried to put an end to the experiment. When an opportunity presented itself, the dogs of the DCRI (the internal security service) were let loose on the farm and the village, and the counter-terrorism apparatus moved in to hammer members of the group one by one. In vain. Though broken up at first by the police operation, communal life has since been rebuilt in Tarnac. More than ever, at the bar-cum-grocer's, old farmers rub shoulders with those not so old who have come from the four corners of the earth. Large meetings are held to think about and discuss the state of the world. Music and cinema are gaining a new lease of life on the plateau. And groups of people from France and abroad, attracted by the example and the promise of friendship, are settling in nearby villages and farms. Activists leave regularly to continue the fight at Notre-Dame-des-Landes or in the Susa Valley, or to block a train carrying nuclear waste in the Cotentin region. Everything is organized without leaders or general assemblies, and with no other means than what they put in themselves. Understandably, the state has tried to stamp out such a dangerous undertaking.

The other example is Marinaleda, an Andalusian village with a population of three thousand. After years of struggle, local peasants and a mayor who has been repeatedly elected for the past thirty years have succeeded in taking over a large farm that used to belong to an aristocratic family. Collectively they now produce there such items as artichokes, sweet peppers and olives. Some work in a cooperative of their own creation, with a canning plant, greenhouses and an olive mill. All the workers receive the same sum: 47 euros a day, or 1,128 euros a month, nearly double the Spanish minimum wage. Rents are 15 euros a month, for 90-square-metre houses with a terrace. And for those who wish to build a home of their own, the municipality offers land, essential materials and the advice of an architect, the only condition being that the future occupant should take part in the construction work. Canteens, school materials, creches and sporting equipment are available free of charge or for a token fee.

The unemployment rate in Marinaleda is zero, whereas the average in the region is around 30 per cent. There is no police – and no crime. Decisions are taken at assemblies that the whole population are invited to attend. The village does not function in egoistic autarky: the mayor and the other inhabitants have more than once joined the struggle of Andalusian farmworkers, distributing food 'levied' from supermarkets, occupying banks, and installing themselves on farmland belonging to the ministry of defence. 'Don't come and tell me that our experience can't be transferred elsewhere,' the mayor says. 'Any town can do the same things if it wants to.'

Tarnac and Marinaleda are islands in the ocean of democratic capitalism. Those who consider the present state of the world to be the only rational one will think that these examples are insignificant. For us, their success and persistence in a hostile environment show that a genuine communism is not only possible but within our reach.

Guillotine. Kolyma. Pol Pot: such is the almost obligatory response to anyone who speaks today of overthrowing the established order. From Hyppolite Taine to Hannah Arendt, many *thinkers* have worked to make the contours of revolution coincide with those of the great bloodbaths, to develop concepts like *totalitarianism* that make it possible to tar everything with the same brush and avoid serious reflection.

The argument does not, however, lack any foundation. In the victorious revolutions of the past, the fate of their opponents has never been enviable, and this is the main and original factor that led those revolutions in the direction we know. Of course, in the French, Russian or Chinese revolutions, the circumstances of the day – civil war, external war – hardly left much latitude to devise solutions other than sheer repression. But there is nothing to suggest that the coming revolution will be immunized *by its nature* against this danger.

Once the state apparatus has broken up, calls for vengeance will be heard from the very first days. Will the arrogance of riches, the hatred and contempt for the people, go unpunished? Will those who organized repression for their own benefit be allowed to eke out their days in peace? However legitimate these questions, however great the pleasure in seeing evil-doers punished, we must say 'no' to the sad passion of revenge. Let us be clear: this has nothing to do with forgiveness, non-violence or any other of those 'values' that were so useful in maintaining the old order. If revenge is to be set aside, it is not for moral reasons.

Against whom should it be exercised? Even if we dismiss personal vendettas that might pollute the legitimate stream of public retribution, the answer is not so simple. Should it be directed at the ministers responsible for years of criminal repression against migrants and the incarceration of their children? Or against the crime squadsters, so reminiscent of wartime collaborationists à la Lacombe Lucien? Or the CEOs who signed off on 'social plans' to improve their company's profitability and increase their bonuses? Or the HR directors who implemented them, or the CRS riot police who gassed those protesting against them? One could easily answer 'yes' to all, but then we'd be talking of hundreds of thousands to be punished. Better in the end to just get on with things: you don't punish a system, you bring it down and leave the fallen debris to its fate.

There is a famous precedent for such a course in Greek antiquity, whose myths and history nevertheless include many varied episodes of revenge. In 403 BCE, the tyranny of the Thirty (imposed on Athens after Sparta's victory in the Peloponnesian war) was ended by the army of Athenian democrats. The overthrow of that cruel and detested regime might have been expected to unleash a wave of collective vengence, but what happened was the opposite. The assembled Athenians took a collective oath *not to recall the evils of the past*. As Nicole Loraux writes in *The Divided City* (Zone Books, 2001): 'Once the tyrants, the same men who had provoked what Cleocritus [the spokesman of the victorious democratic army] described as "the most awful war, the most sacrilegious, the most odious to gods and men", are expelled, once they are charged with all the crimes of which Athens must be exonerated, after all this, well, let's forget it! Officially and institutionally.

Forget that there were two parties; and the winners themselves solicit the forgetting, those same men who had knowingly chosen their side.'

One might fear that such an amnesty would make more people than ever thirst for revenge, as Nietzsche once suggested. But no, there will be enough joyful sights to ward off frustration and to dispel resentment: for example, yesterday's powerful men carrying their shopping in plastic bags, at Gennevilliers station on the bleak outskirts of Paris; the children of poor neighbourhoods playing in the gardens of former ministries; police stations converted into recording studios, and yachts into sailing schools for schoolchildren.

What the victorious revolution should establish is the exact opposite of collective punishment: real liberty. The most novel and surprising developments will be in the means of expression. Of course, 'free expression' is the grand theme that makes today's democracies so self-satisfied, allowing them to present themselves as the lesser evil. And it is true that in France you can say almost anything without risk, and that since the Algerian war there have been no censors. But the simple reason for this is that *there has been nothing to censor.*

In the industrialized world, virtually all printed newspapers, nine-tenths of publishing and most audiovisual output are owned by financiers. And at the head of their employees in information and entertainment, they have placed reliable men (sometimes women) trained in the economics and business schools, who have no need of directives to follow the general line reflecting the political consensus and competitive commercial considerations. Such people are judged by figures – audience share, print runs, advertising revenue – and any thanks they receive is for their performance on these points, not for a sudden flash of independence.

Appointed by the owners of capital, these authorized representatives install beneath them others whose docility can be guaranteed; the process is then repeated all the way down the company hierarchy, or at least as far as the technical personnel, who on the whole have their own views on matters. Thus, far more than a cynical wish to misinform and dumb-down, it is institutional conformism and voluntary servitude that make media products so massively uninteresting. The public is aware of this – which does much more than vague anthropological or cultural considerations to account for the 'crisis' of the press, book publishing, and so on.

To liberate information and permit the free expression of opinions is therefore not the same as doing away with a surveillance that has no need to exist. To depose the media bosses and dismiss the hierarchy are an indispensable first step, but the logical continuation – to hand the press and audiovisual media over to those who work in them – is not a matter of course. Most of the journalists in question have been formed (formatted) in the grey world of political science faculties. Coming from the same intellectual and political background, they *believe* what they write – that Camus is a great philosopher, that Pope Francis stands up for the poor, or that Areva, the French multinational energy group, is an industry flagship unjustifiably targeted by terrorists. With some exceptions, the media teams already in place will not bring even a breath of fresh air to the world of information. At the same time, we should not forget that for a long period in history those who wrote in the press were not always professional news-papermen. Neither Marat nor Zola nor Orwell was a 'journalist', and the same is true of the authors of today's rare articles of interest. We shall go further in this direction; we shall open up the press and audio-visual media to *everyone* – to those whose voices are never heard, but also to those who disagree (whether they regret the passing of the old order or are impa-tient to see the new course speed up). There will be acceptance of do-it-yourself broadcasts, imperfec-tions, gaps and heterogeneity. There will be no longing for classroom voices, slick hypocrisy, uniformly dull editorials, or the idiotic games that make up today's bleak 'media landscape'.

But it is not only a matter of the expression of ideas: a counter-revolution will unfailingly seek to organize itself. It is impossible to predict the conspiracies and stratagems that it will come up with to restore capitalism, or the counter-blows that will be necessary to oppose it. We can only say that we will not reopen the gates of the prisons we have just pulled down, that we will neither banish nor execute our enemies. Let us trust in the collective imagination: that is what is most cruelly lacking amid the fog of democratic capitalism. 'You have seen an immense people, master of its destiny, return to order amid all the fallen powers – powers that have oppressed it for so many centuries' (Robespierre, *Contre la loi martiale*, 22 February 1790).

In the world of democratic capitalism, philosophy, literature, cinema and various kinds of art fare worse than they did twenty or thirty years ago. Rampant commodification has transformed culture into a set of *contents*, a reservoir of *products*, whose success depends on their profitability. In France, the large publishing houses have been turned into façades, like buildings whose old exterior stones and mouldings have been preserved, but whose interiors have been gutted to give way to glassed open spaces and air-conditioned offices. Behind the glorious names – Calmann-Lévy, Fayard, Plon or Flammarion – one finds financiers and businessmen in command, and often, right at the top, clowns like the famous Jean-Marie Messier or, today, Arnaud Lagardère. Best-selling authors are bought and exchanged like footballers. Léautaud at Mercure de France, Paulhan and Queneau at Gallimard are legends from another age. Just as motor cars can now be told apart only by the shape of their lights, there is little to distinguish the books produced by industrial publishers other than their cover designs. (The difference between the auto industry and publishing is that minor car makers such as Studebaker, Delage or Salmson disappeared long ago, whereas more or less everywhere a plethora of small houses, some of them really tiny, manage to publish most of what is worth reading.)

In the United States, the large galleries handle sums of money that raise them to the level of industry, and their branches all around the world disseminate the methods of art marketing. What sells best, as in literature, is a flouting of the same traditional 'values' that wealthy purchasers apply every day of the week. Today's industrial culture, a pathetic caricature of the literary and artistic avant-gardes of the early twentieth century, operates on the appearance of challenging the existing order of things – an order of which it is itself one of the main pillars. Indeed, the very word *criticism*, which has been hijacked by the fake left as much as by the genuine right, should arouse the greatest suspicion in spite of its noble genealogy.

After the work of dismantling has taken place, the drudges crammed four into an office, who have kept their freedom of thought, will take the book orders and easily run the new small publishing houses, given that it was they (women more often than men) who did the real work while leaving the members of reading committees and all manner of businessmen and communicators to parade centre-stage before the public. At the same time, new exhibition sites, new ways of producing films, new readers and new audiences will spring up on all sides. The disappearance of the university, the great agent of present-day sterility, will release energies and talents for something better than the editing of articles intended to enable their authors to rise up the mandarinate hierarchy.

This *cultural revolution* will not automatically bring geniuses to light. But history tells us that times of collective joy, when subjectivities are dazzled by a sense of participation in a common adventure, are also the ones of greatest creativity.

3

THERE'S EVERYTHING
TO PLAY FOR

Frivolity and again ennui, which are spreading
in the established order of things, the undefined
foreboding of something unknown – all these
betoken that there is something else approaching.
This gradual crumbling to pieces, which did not
alter the general look and aspect of the whole, is
interrupted by the sunrise, which, in a flash and
at a single stroke, brings to view the form
and structure of the new world.

Hegel, Preface to *The Phenomenology of Mind*
(Baillie translation)

The dislocated history of our times, bringing the collapse of many dreams and a series of setbacks in what used to be called the Third World, has scotched the idea that things are evolving by a kind of inner necessity towards major advances in liberty and equality. Although the class struggle everywhere continues in various forms, its outcome is nowhere assured. In his despairing *Theses on the Philosophy of History*, written in 1940, Walter Benjamin already questioned the concept of a meaning of history and saw 'a storm blowing' which 'is what we call progress'.

We know all that postmodern nihilism has been able to draw from such questioning: a militant apology for resignation, the disarming of nascent energies, a cultivated version of counter-revolution. For us, the present is to be analysed in strategic terms, and it is essential to observe how our enemies are already arming themselves against the impending upheaval.

Recently, fascism has often been mentioned as one possibility in the form of a 'return to the thirties'. The word is convenient but not correct: the reference to fascist movements of the interwar period does not enable us to grasp the real danger ahead, since what characterized those movements – the Leader cult, jackbooted troops, an emphasis on martial heroism, the ideology of the irrational – is no longer part of our times. Rather than of fascism, one might speak of a process of fascistoid impregnation, in countries where trust and respect for the rulers, 'elites', parties and trade unions have broken down. This draws its virulence from a hatred of foreigners: Turks in Germany and the Nordic countries, Romanians in Hungary, Albanians in Italy, Arabs and blacks in France, Chicanos in the United States, Roma everywhere.

In France, racist discourse is said to be 'shedding its complexes' – a curious notion that tends to make of it a deep instinct hitherto misguidedly bottled up. Politicians, journalists and writers commonly say things that, not so long ago, would have forced them into a public apology. Michel Houellebecq, for example, wrote: 'Islam could only have been born in a stupid desert, amid filthy bedouins who had nothing better to do – pardon me – than bugger their camels' (*The Possibility of an Island*, 2006), and received the Prix Goncourt (Céline only ever got the Renaudot prize). Following the law of 2005 that emphasized the positive side of colonization, primary schoolchildren have been handed the sentences of Jules Ferry on superior races, which 'have a right vis-à-vis inferior races because there is a duty towards them. They have a duty to civilize inferior races.'

This would already be worrying if it were just a question of words. But in many countries, we see the spread of violent groups that specialize in hunting people with dark skins – or even light skins if they are followers of the Muslim religion. Of course the far right has always had its thugs, but 'the crisis' has added something new by giving a place to such movements operating within the parliamentary system, from the American Tea Party to the French Front National, a place that unnerves our rulers: right-wing political oneupmanship is the counter-blow they have come up with to block the way for 'populism'. Their police apparatus closes its eyes to racist crimes, when it does not actually work in concert with far-right gangs to make their order prevail.

In Athens, Golden Dawn makes no secret of its pedigree: 'Hitler was a great social reformist and a great organizer of the social state,' its current spokeman declared (as quoted in issue number 7 of the magazine *Z*). The armed wing of the movement – which calls itself 'Security Battalions', an allusion to a wartime force that collaborated with the Nazis – patrols the popular districts with a high immigrant population, checking, attacking and pillaging with impunity. Indeed, far from intervening, the police collaborates with the militias, assigns them to keep order in rough areas, and joins forces with them to beat up immigrants and those who support them. In the grand tradition of modern Greece, from Metaxas to the Colonels, the state apparatus relies on Golden Dawn to contain the popular movement. In Germany, faced with a series of murders of Turks (and Greeks) holding doner kebabs, the police for ten years pretended to believe that they were a settling of scores among the Turkish drug mafia. The truth only came out by chance: that is, the killers belonged to a neo-Nazi group called the Nationalsozialistischer Untergrund (NSU). In France, far-right infiltration of the security apparatus is a longstanding tradition, but we have never before heard an interior minister making racist remarks in public – the jokes of Hortefeux on the right; or the assertions of Manuel Valls on the left, who thinks it would be good 'to put whites back on their feet in [the Paris suburb] Evry', and who orders the dismantling of Roma camps because 'they don't want to integrate into our country [and] are run by networks well versed in begging and prostitution'. (One can imagine this Socialist following the same kind of trajectory as Marcel Déat who, at the SFIO Congress in 1933, launched the slogan 'Order, Authority, Nation', before splitting away to found the Rassemblement National Populaire, a genuinely fascist party.) We also have to reckon with the red-brown plague of Alain Soral and his people, which is wreaking havoc among the Catholic bourgeoisie as well as the most disoriented 'suburban youth'.

Against this drift, 'anti-fascism' is an illusory path to follow. Although it may become necessary to form local self-defence groups, the meetings where intellectual 'personalities' come to express their indignation are like advance signs of defeat; one is reminded of photos of the Writers' Congress for the Defence of Culture in 1935, where the looming disaster can be read on the pathetic faces of Gide, Benda, Ehrenburg and Barbusse. In France today, marked by the intense propaganda on the internet of Soral's Equality and Reconciliation group, by the reconstitution of Nazi skinhead gangs and even by the murder of left-wing activists (one of the most notorious being that of Clément Méric in June 2013), anti-fascism has once again become a diversion. Since fascism feeds on hatred of democratic corruption, the anti-fascist response gives it additional strength by conveying an impression of support for the existing democratic order. It is the revolutionary upsurge, the 'fraternal awakening of all energies' (to quote Rimbaud), which will send the fascist apprentices packing.

Apart from 'fascism', the other possibility – which does not preclude various fascistic thrusts – is a continuing breakdown of social, cultural and governmental infrastructures that never reaches completion: a kind of end without an ending, which no revolutionary or counter-revolutionary surge ever quite wraps up; an infinite degradation of everything; a dissolution of the present order without an explosion. Such a process is imaginable because of the new and diffuse cybernetic control of whole populations, and because, beyond the vanishing of any society worthy of the name, Google, Facebook, Apple, Microsoft and co. maintain a semblance of social relations, a 'social network'. The former boss of Google, Eric Schmidt, explains in a book he wrote with an American anti-terrorist agent (*The New Digital Age*, 2013) that Somalia is a fascinating textbook case since it is the oldest of the 'failed states' – a country where any form of state disappeared way back in 1991. Nothing works in Somalia except for telecommunications, which are less expensive there than anywhere else; failing an adequate food ration, a quarter of Somalis possess a mobile phone. Similarly, at the 'end' of the war in Iraq, the supply of water, food and medicine could not be relied upon anywhere, but everyone carried a mobile phone. The dream scenario for Google and its ilk is for smartphones and myriad apps to provide all the 'services' that the state is no longer in a position to supply: access to education, information, banks, weather forecasts, and so on. Here the collapse becomes a stable condition – and a profitable one.

For Europe, a Somali scenario is not to be feared in the immediate future. It is a variant that needs to be borne in mind: on the one hand, ever richer, ever more 'communicative', ever more global, connected and productive city centres; on the other hand, more and more nightmarish zones of banishment, where everything is in short supply, where all trace of the state has disappeared, where people survive only through 'crime' before dying an early and brutal death, where regular 'anti-terrorist' operations and army incursions permit constant disorganization and ultimately make it possible to render chaos inoffensive. The 'networked metropolis' might then look at itself through the eyes of its opposite and pass off its deep-rooted barbarism as a peak of civilization. In those banishment areas, as in Somalia, telecommunications could easily be kept in service, especially as they would allow constant monitoring of all exchanges and relationships formed there – a continual flow of information to those who 'run' the business from their comfortable position outside. You would thus have the maintenance of capitalism through ultra-profitable interconnected pockets, together with optimal management of its contradictions and the threat represented by brutal impoverishment of the greatest number. The rulers would not forget to denounce the inexplicable 'descent of the population into savagery', and they might even point to racial causes for the catastrophic situation they have deliberately produced.

This is why we cannot merely watch and *record* the collapse of the present social edifice; we must make it happen as soon as possible, before a permanent state of decomposition has been established. Blanqui: 'Only the Revolution, by clearing the ground, will light up the horizon and open the roads, or rather the many paths, that lead towards the new order.'

So as not to find ourselves stuck in one or another version of the life-and-death struggle waged by democratic capitalism, the first idea is *to organize*. If the current ferment remains fragmented, if the centres of revolt are linked by nothing other than mutual sympathy, the state apparatus will continue to stand, even if only a layer of rust holds it together. But the word *organization* sometimes takes on a magical character, by covering practices that are largely a matter for the imagination.

To rebuild a classical revolutionary organization on the ruins of the past is neither possible nor desirable. It is not possible because in the end no one wants it, except for members of the little neo-Trotskyist, neo-Leninist or neo-Maoist groups that line trade union processions and offer their newspapers written in a language from another age. And it is not desirable because its implicit aim could only be a head-on confrontation with the state apparatus, which will never take place because the 'objective conditions' will never be present. Such an organization can therefore lead its troops only into a garrulous wait-and-see policy – or perhaps one day into a suicidal action.

We must start from what we have before our eyes, not from some fantasy projection. Everyone can see groups of people – wage earners and unemployed, soup kitchen users, prisoners, single mothers – who can no longer endure the life they are forced to lead. Everyone can hear the anger in the factories, popular suburbs and ports, among megastore cashiers and Orange employees, in the banks and newspapers, even among airline pilots. To organize means to help these groups evolve gradually into subversive constellations through the force of friendships, shared hopes and common struggles. It means to open up paths that help them to get together across towns and villages, between one neighbourhood and another, from city centre to outlying *banlieue*. That is the opposite of the abstract 'convergence of struggles' that professional activists always invoke but never achieve. The only convergence of struggles we can imagine is *local or regional*: a struggle in a tyre factory – Continental at Clairvoix, for example – could carry along the whole surrounding area, where everyone's lives would be affected by its victory or defeat. Instead of living as if enrolled in a given sector of the economy, instead of seeking to converge with struggles in the same sector in the four corners of the country or continent, a factory could also think of itself as immersed in a whole set of local links, which the conflict has every chance of politicizing *because it affects them directly*.

In the same way, it is not our business to explain to the downtrodden why they are downtrodden and how they can escape their condition. The coming revolution will have no vanguard, only liaison men and women who work to kindle and spread revolutionary futures. 'Pessimism of the intellect', Gramsci wrote, and we have seen the results. In a world that is cracking at the seams, pessimism does no more than intensify the death that is already under way.

So, there we are. Since time is pressing, let us press forward, measure our strength, and meet up with one another.